worship BAND PLAY-ALONG

BASS EDITION **Volume 1**

Holy Is the Lord

BASS

Recorded and produced by Jim Reith at BeatHouse Music, Milwaukee, WI

Lead Vocals by Tonia Emrich and Jim Reith
Background Vocals by Jim Reith and Jana Wolf
Guitars by Mike DeRose
Bass by Chris Kringel
Piano by Kurt Cowling
Drums by Del Bennett

ISBN-13: 978-1-4234-1714-9
ISBN-10: 1-4234-1714-3

HAL•LEONARD® CORPORATION

7777 W. BLUEMOUND RD. P.O. BOX 13819 MILWAUKEE, WI 53213

Visit Hal Leonard Online at
www.halleonard.com

Holy Is the Lord

Agnus Dei

Words and Music by Michael W. Smith

Chorus 1

Verse

Be Unto Your Name

Words and Music by Lynn DeShazo and Gary Sadler

might-y to ___ save. ___ You are the love ___ song we'll sing for-ev ___ - er, bow-ing be-fore ___ You,

Chorus

bless-ing Your name. _____ Ho - ly, ho - ly, Lord God Al - might - y,

Wor - thy is the Lamb who was slain. High-est prais - es, hon - or and glo-

- ry be un - to Your ___ name, _____ be un -

*D played on low B string.

God of Wonders

Words and Music by Marc Byrd and Steve Hindalong

ho - ly. ___ The u-ni-verse___ de-clares___ Your maj-es - ty. You are

Bridge

ho - ly, ___ ho - ly, ___ Hal-le - lu - jah to the

Lord ___ of ___ heav-en and ___ earth. ___ Hal-le - lu - jah to the Lord ___ of ___ heav-en and ___ earth. ___

___ Hal-le - lu - jah to the Lord ___ of ___ heav-en and ___ earth. ___ Hal-le - lu - jah to the

Outro

Holy Is the Lord

Words and Music by Chris Tomlin and Louie Giglio

Chorus

Ho - ly is the Lord ___ God ___ Al - might-

- y. The ___ earth ___ is filled ___ with His glo -

- ry. Ho - ly is the Lord ___ God ___ Al - might -

- y. The _ earth ___ is filled _ with His glo - ry, the _ earth _

Chorus

It Is You

Words and Music by Peter Furler

God Al - might - y _____ and ho - ly, ho - ly is His _____

Bridge

_____ name a - lone. ___ As we lift _____ up our hands, ___ as we call _

_____ on Your name, ___ will You vis - it this place ___ by Your mer -

- cy and grace? ___ As we lift _____ up our hands, ___ as we call _

Chorus

Chorus

Open the Eyes of My Heart

Words and Music by Paul Baloche

O - pen the eyes __ of my heart, __ Lord. _____ O - pen the eyes __ of my heart. __

__ I want to see You, _____ I want to

Chorus

see You. _____ To see You high and lift - ed up,

shin - ing in the light of Your glo - ry.

Chorus

high and lift - ed up, shin -

- ing in the light of Your glo - ry.

Pour out Your pow - er and love as we sing

ho - ly, ho - ly, ho - ly. To see You

We Fall Down

Words and Music by Chris Tomlin

We fall ___ down, ___ we ___ lay our _____ crowns ___ at the feet ___ of Je -

- sus. The great - ness ___ of ___ mer - cy and ___ love ___ at the feet ___

You Are Holy

(Prince of Peace)

Words and Music by Marc Imboden and Tammi Rhoton

AGNUS DEI

MICHAEL W. SMITH

Key of **G Major, 4/4**

VERSE:

Gsus2 G C/G G C/G   G
Al   - le - lu - ia

G C/G G C/G D/G C/G
Al - le - lu - ia

**   D/G   C/G   G**
For the Lord God Almighty reigns

G C/G G C/G   G
Al   - le - lu - ia

G C/G G C/G D/G C/G
Al - le - lu - ia

**   D/G   C/G   G**
For the Lord God Almighty reigns

G C/G G C/G D/G C/G
Al - le - lu - ia

CHORUS 1:

C/G D/F♯ G
Ho   -   ly

D/F♯   G(add2)
Ho - ly

**   C/G G   Em   D**
Are You, Lord God Almight - y

**   C(add2)**
Worthy is the Lamb

**   C**
Worthy is the Lamb

C D Gsus2
A - men

(REPEAT VERSE)

CHORUS 2:

C/E D/G G
Ho -   ly

D/G   G
Ho - ly

**   C/G G   Em   D**
Are You, Lord God Almight - y

**   C(add2)**
Worthy is the Lamb

**   C(add2)**
Worthy is the Lamb

**   G**
You are ho - ly

D/G   G
Ho - ly

**   C/G G   Em   D**
Are You, Lord God Almight - y

**   C**
Worthy is the Lamb

**   C**
Worthy is the Lamb

C D Gsus2
A - men

BE UNTO YOUR NAME

LYNN DESHAZO and GARY SADLER

Key of **A Major, 3/4**

INTRO:

A E Bm F#m D Asus A Esus E

VERSE 1:

A   E   Bm   F#m
We are a moment, You are forever

D   A/C# G   E
Lord of the ages,   God before time

A   E   Bm   F#m
We are a vapor, You are eternal

D   A/C# G   Esus E
Love everlasting, reigning on high

CHORUS:

F#m D A/C#   A
Holy, Holy, Lord God Almighty

F#m   D   A   E
Worthy is the Lamb who was slain

F#m   D   A/C#   E
Highest praises, honor and glory

Bm F#m   Esus E
   Be unto Your name

Bm F#m   Esus E
   Be unto Your name

VERSE 2:

A   E   Bm   F#m
We are the broken, You are the healer

D   A/C# G   E
Jesus, Redeemer, mighty to save

A   E   Bm   F#m
You are the love song we'll sing forever

D   A/C# G   Esus E
Bowing before You, blessing Your name.

(REPEAT CHORUS 2X)

TAG:

Bm   F#m   Esus E
   Be unto Your name

Bm   F#m   Esus E (hold)
   Be unto Your name

GOD OF WONDERS

MARC BYRD and STEVE HINDALONG

Key of **G Major, 4/4**

VERSE 1:

Dsus   **Em7**   **Csus2**
Lord of all creation

Dsus   **Em**   **Csus2**
Of water, earth and sky

Dsus   **Em**   **Csus2**
The heavens are Your tabernacle

Dsus   **Em**   **Csus2**
Glory to the Lord on high

CHORUS:

G   **Dsus D**
God of wonders beyond our galaxy

       Am7   **Csus2**
You are holy,   holy

   G   **Dsus D**
The universe declares Your majesty

     Am7   **Csus2**
You are holy,   holy

Csus2   **Csus2(add#4)**
Lord of heaven and earth

C   **Csus2(add#4)**
Lord of heaven and earth

VERSE 2:

Dsus **Em7**   **Csus2**
Early in the morning

Dsus   **Em**   **Csus2**
I will celebrate the light

Dsus **Em7**   **C**
And as I stumble in the darkness

Dsus   **Em7**   **Csus2**
I will call Your name by   night

(REPEAT CHORUS)

BRIDGE:

Am7   **Cmaj7**
Hallelujah to the Lord of heaven and earth

Am7   **Cmaj7**
Hallelujah to the Lord of heaven and earth

Am7   **Cmaj7**
Hallelujah to the Lord of heaven and earth

Am7   **Cmaj7**
Hallelujah to the Lord of heaven and earth

Dsus   **D**

CHORUS:

G   **Dsus D**
God of wonders beyond our galaxy

       Am7   **Csus2**
You are holy,   holy

   G   **Dsus D**
The universe declares Your majesty

     Am7   **Csus2**
You are holy,   holy

Csus2   **Csus2(add#4)**
Lord of heaven and earth

C   **Csus2(add#4)**
Lord of heaven and earthC

C(add2)   **Csus2(add#4)**
Lord of heaven and earth

HOLY IS THE LORD

CHRIS TOMLIN and LOUIE GIGLIO

Key of **G Major**, 4/4

INTRO (GUITAR ONLY):

G Csus2 D

G Csus2 D

VERSE:

G   Csus2   D
We stand and lift up our hands

      G/B   Csus2   D
For the joy of the Lord is our strength

G   Csus2   D
We bow down and worship Him now

G/B   Csus2   D
How great, how awesome is He

       A7sus   Csus2
Together we sing

CHORUS:

       G/B Csus2 Dsus D
Holy is the Lord God Almighty

   Em7   Csus2   Dsus
The earth is filled with His glory

D   G/B Csus2 Dsus   D
Holy is the Lord God Almighty

   Em7   Csus2   Dsus D
The earth is filled with His glory

   Em7   Csus2   Dsus D
The earth is filled with His glory

(REPEAT VERSE & CHORUS)

BRIDGE:

   G   D/F♯
It's rising up all around

       F   C
It's the anthem of the Lord's renown

   G   D/F♯
It's rising up all around

      F   C
It's the anthem of the Lord's renown

          A7sus   Cadd2
And together we sing

      A7sus   Cadd2
Everyone sing

(REPEAT CHORUS)

(REPEAT LAST LINE OF CHORUS)

END ON G

IT IS YOU

Peter Furler

Key of **G Major**, 4/4

INTRO:

Em C D　　**Em C D**

VERSE:

Em　　**C**　　　　**D**
As we lift up our hands, will You meet us here

Em　　**C**　　　　**D**
As we call on Your name, will You meet us here

Em　　　**C**　　　　　**D**
We have come to this place to worship You

Em　　　**C**　　　　**D**
God of mercy and grace

PRE-CHORUS:

　　G　　**C**
It is You we adore

　　G　　　　　**C**
It is You praises are for

　　G　　　　　　　**C**
Only You the heavens declare

　　G　　　**C**
It is You, it is You

CHORUS:

D　　　　　　　**C**　　**G**
And holy, holy is our God Almighty

D　　　　　　　**C**　　**G**
And holy, holy is His name alone

D　　　　　　　**C**　　**G**
And holy, holy is our God Almighty

D　　　　　　　**C**　　**G**
And holy, holy is His name alone

TRANSITION BACK TO VERSE:

　　G　　　　**C**
It is You we adore

　　　　G　　　　　**C**
It is You, only You

(REPEAT VERSE, PRE-CHORUS & CHORUS)

BRIDGE:

G　　　**D**
As we lift up our hands

　　　　C　　　　**G**
As we call on Your name

　　　　　　D
Will You visit this place

　　　　　C　　　　**G**
By Your mercy and grace

　　　　　　D
As we lift up our hands

　　　　C　　　　**G**
As we call on Your name

　　　　　　D
Will You visit in this place

　　　　　C　　　　**G**
By Your mercy and grace

G　　　　**C**
It is You we adore

　　G　　　**C**
It is You, it is You

(REPEAT CHORUS 2X)

ENDING:

　　G　　　**C**
It is You we adore

　　G　　　　**C** (hold)
It is You, only You

OPEN THE EYES OF MY HEART

PAUL BALOCHE

Key of **D Major, 4/4**

INTRO (FOUR BARS):

Dsus2

VERSE:

D
Open the eyes of my heart, Lord

A/D
Open the eyes of my heart

      G/D
I want to see You

    D
I want to see You

(REPEAT VERSE)

CHORUS:

       A   **Bm**
To see You high and lifted up

G   **A**
Shining in the light of Your glory

A   **Bm**
Pour out Your power and love

      G   **A**
As we sing holy, holy, holy

(REPEAT VERSE 2X)

(REPEAT CHORUS 2X)

VERSE (2X):

D
Holy, holy holy

A/C♯
Holy, holy, holy

G/B   **G**
Holy, holy, holy

        D
I want to see You

TAG (2X):

D/F♯   **G**   **D**
I want to see You, I want to see You

WE FALL DOWN

CHRIS TOMLIN

Key of **D Major**, 4/4

INTRO (FOUR BARS):

D   A Bm G(add2)

VERSE:

D   A   Bm
We fall down, we lay our crowns

      G   Em7(add4)
At the feet of Jesus

     D   A   Bm
The greatness of mercy and love

     G   G/A A
At the feet of Jesus

CHORUS:

     D/F♯   G   D/F♯ Em7
And we cry holy, holy, holy

D/F♯   G   D/F♯ Em7
We cry holy, holy, holy

Bm A G   D/F♯ Em7
We cry holy, holy, holy

Asus D Dsus A Bm
Is the Lamb

G(add2) Em7(add4)

(REPEAT VERSE)

CHORUS:

    D/F♯   G   D/F♯ Em7
And we cry holy, holy, holy

D/F♯   G   D/F♯ Em7
We cry holy, holy, holy

Bm A G   D/F♯ Em7
We cry holy, holy, holy

Asus A D   Dsus D
Is   the Lamb

CHORUS:

Em7   D/F♯ G   D/F♯ Em7
And we cry   holy, holy, holy

D/F♯   G   D/F♯ Em7
We cry holy, holy, holy

Bm A G   D/F♯ Em7
We cry holy, holy, holy

Asus A D
Is   the Lamb

A Bm G Asus A D

YOU ARE HOLY (PRINCE OF PEACE)

MARC IMBODEN and TAMMI RHOTON

Key of **G Major**, 4/4

INTRO (EIGHT BARS):

G   G/C   Dsus D Dsus2 D

G   G/C   Dsus D Dsus2 D

VERSE:

     G(add2)   *Echo:*
You are holy   *(You are holy)*

     C(add2)
You are mighty   *(You are mighty)*

    Am7
You are worthy   *(You are worthy)*

     D
Worthy of praise *(worthy of praise)*

    G(add2)
I will follow   *(I will follow)*

    C(add2)2
I will listen   *(I will listen)*

    Am7
I will love You   *(I will love You)*

D **G**   **D**   **G**
All of my days *(all of my days)*

CHORUS
(Part I and Part II sung simultaneously):

PART I

    Csus2   **Dsus**
I will sing to and worship

   Em7   **G/B**
The King who is worthy

     Csus2   **Dsus**
And I will love and adore Him

      Em7   **G/B**
And I will bow down before Him

     Csus2   **Dsus**
And I will sing to and worship

   Em7   **G/B**
The King who is worthy

     Csus2   **Dsus**
And I will love and adore Him

      Em7   **Asus** **A**
And I will bow down before Him

     C(add2)
You're my Prince of Peace

      D   **G**
And I will live my life for You.

PART II

    Csus2   **Dsus**
You are Lord of lords, You are King of kings

   Em7   **G/B**
You are mighty God, Lord of everything

     Csus2   **D**
You're Emmanuel, You're the Great I AM

      Em7   **G/B**
You're the Prince of Peace, who is the Lamb

     Csus2   **Dsus**
You're the Living God, You're my saving grace

      Em7   **G/B**
You will reign forever, You are Ancient of Days

     Csus2   **Dsus**
You are Alpha, Omega, Beginning and End

      Em7   **Asus**   **A**
You're my Savior, Messiah, Redeemer and Friend

     C(add2)
You're my Prince of Peace

      D   **G**
And I will live my life for You

(REPEAT VERSE)

(REPEAT CHORUS 2X)

TAG:

     Csus2
You're my Prince of Peace

      D   **G**
And I will live my life for You